HUDSON BAY
BRITISH CANADA
ALBANY RIVER
MOOSE RIVER
LAKE NIPIGON
MISSINAIBI RIVER
LAKE ABITIBI
FORT WILLIAM
LAKE SUPERIOR
LAKE NIPISSING
OTTAWA RIVER
FRENCH R.
QUEBEC
ST. LAWRENCE RIVER
MONTREAL
LACHINE
LAKE HURON
LAKE MICHIGAN
WISCONSIN RIVER
LAKE ONTARIO
FORT NIAGARA
FORT DETROIT
LAKE ERIE
ATLANTIC OCEAN
To Neil
I enjoyed your company
I don't believe you're 71. I wish you many happy adventures.
Steve
Steve Johnson
2127 Echo Tr.
Ely, MN 55731

THE ILLUSTRATED VOYAGEUR

Paintings and Companion Stories
by Howard Sivertson

Midwest Traditions
Mount Horeb, Wisconsin
1994

Midwest Traditions, Inc. is a nonprofit educational organization devoted to the study and preservation of the folk arts and traditional cultures of the American Midwest. Our publications serve to bring this rich, diverse heritage to broader public attention.

For a free catalog of books and other materials, write:
Midwest Traditions
P.O. Box 320
Mount Horeb, WI 53572
(or call toll-free 1-800-736-9189)

Special thanks to the Wisconsin Arts Board, State of Wisconsin, and to the Friends of Midwest Traditions for support to help establish this cultural publishing effort.

ISBN: 1-883953-05-7
Library of Congress Catalog Card #94-75122

Manufactured in the United States of America
Printed on acid-free paper
This is printing number: 10 9 8 7 6 5 4 3 2 1

Book Design: Lisa Teach-Swaziek, PeachTree Design
Editor: Philip Martin
Printer: Park Printing House, Ltd.
Color Separations: Four Lakes Colorgraphics Inc.
Binding: R & R Bindery

Publisher's Cataloging in Publication

Sivertson, Howard, 1930-
The illustrated voyageur / Howard Sivertson.
p. cm.
Includes bibliographical references.
ISBN 1-883953-05-7

1. Fur trade–Great Lakes Region–History–Pictorial works. 2. Fur traders–Travel–Great Lakes Region–History–Pictorial works. 3. Canoes and canoeing–Great Lakes Region–History–Pictorial works. I. Title.

F1060.8.S55 1994 971.3'0088639'1
QBI94-87

Acknowledgements

The paintings in this book are reproduced courtesy of the artist; any unauthorized reproduction is strictly prohibited.

A few of the paintings are on public display. Special thanks to the Grand Portage National Monument ("The Annual Cycle," p. 6, and "Grand Portage Stockade in 1792," p. 37), to the Grand Portage Lodge & Casino ("Sabbath Sunrise," p. 41 and "Brigade from Montreal," p. 18). Most of the other paintings are currently in individual collections.

Permission to quote from the diaries of John Macdonell and Archibald N. McLeod, published by the Minnesota Historical Society Press in the book *Five Fur Traders of the Northwest,* Charles M. Gates, ed., 1965, is gratefully acknowledged.

This book would not have been possible without the kind help of many others. We would especially like to thank Jon Sage of Grand Portage National Monument, and Joe Winterburn and Jean Morrison of Old Fort William, for their comments on early versions of the manuscript.

Table of Contents

Introduction

I am not sure whether I became an artist in response to my love for the Lake Superior area where I was raised, or if I was born an artist and have stayed to live and paint here because of the area's natural beauty.

I was born in 1930 during the Great Depression and was raised on Lake Superior's Isle Royale and Minnesota's North Shore.

The natural settings of the western Lake Superior region where I grew up—including the nearby Boundary Waters/Quetico canoe wilderness—are still my favorite places. This region and its peoples are also the source of inspiration for my paintings. My first book, *Once Upon An Isle*, was a collection of autobiographical paintings and recollections about growing up in a fishing family on Isle Royale.

For my father and the other Isle Royale fishermen and their families, daily life was fraught with uncertainty, discomfort, and danger at times. But we were always surrounded by the great beauty of the wilderness landscape.

In the same vein, for many years now I have studied, pondered, and painted scenes of earlier travelers and inhabitants who first encountered this wilderness of inland lakes, remote islands, river waterways, and endless forests.

As I sat on the ancient portage trails in the Boundary Waters Canoe Area, I often imagined a brigade of 18th-century voyageurs paddling down the lake, traveling over the portages, or stopping to eat their "rubbaboo" soup. While combing the beaches of Isle Royale, I wondered what a caribou hunt by early Indian visitors to the island looked like. Steering my father's small boat to the nets, I would picture in my mind the voyageur fishermen, employed by the American Fur Company to harvest trout and whitefish from Lake Superior waters.

The wakes of the birchbark canoes have long since calmed. The footprints of voyageur moccasins on portage trails have vanished. The fragile watercraft, the transcontinental journeys, the rendezvous and revelry of the canoemen of the late 1700s are gone and easily forgotten in the distance of time. My curiosity about who they were and how their travels appeared led me to research and paint these scenes as best I could.

Certainly, like most who look back into history, I am guilty of the idealism of my modern-day opinions. The enthusiasm I feel as a 20th-century artist in the wilderness, traveling old waterways and trails, totally free to choose my own directions, is a wonderful way to reflect on the heritage of this region... with my sketchbook, modern canoe, and freeze-dried foods.

Any desire to return to the days of the voyageurs is dampened by the thought, for instance, of the crude, painful, and often-deadly medical technology of that era.

Starvation, freezing to death, and other dangers come to mind quickly enough to deter my desire to journey into the past.

But the more I think about those risks, the more respect and admiration I have for the hardy, self-reliant voyageurs who had the guts and determination to survive and travel thousands of miles through these wild places.

I believe the essence of wilderness is freedom. The earliest explorers or traders had a certain freedom to journey at their own pace, to choose their own trails, to take whatever risks seemed prudent, so long as they heeded the basic rules of nature and the dictates of supplies and their rudimentary equipment.

As the fur trade grew, the wilderness became more and more something that the wealthy and powerful sought to regulate and rule. Delivery schedules and profits, markets and shareholder interests began to dictate the flow of human activity through the wilderness. Poorly paid, often in debt to the company, the hardworking canoemen surely did not equate wilderness with recreation. They had to follow a prescribed route with a pressing time schedule imposed, allowing few luxuries of rest or enjoyment. The voyageur awakened early before sunrise, paddled all day with few breaks, and went to sleep on the hard ground.

Yet, the era of the voyageurs of the North West Company and their long canoe travels was a fascinating episode in the history of the north. In these decades at the end of the 18th century, wilderness was considered important to businessman and backwoodsman alike. Wild regions were necessary to the fur trade for animal habitat. Great reaches of forest and prairie allowed and encouraged the Native American families to hunt, travel, and trade with the fur-trade posts—the more isolated a post, the better for business.

The voyageurs passed back and forth through a tremendous northern wilderness, one of the most beautiful areas of the world. For weeks and months at a time, the canoemen of the late 1700s were exposed to great beauty. What did they see in the wilderness through which they traveled? How did they respond? What were their thoughts?

This we cannot know. Unable to read or write, the voyageurs left virtually no written records, only a rich oral tradition of French-Canadian paddling songs handed down over generations. We have just a few reflections by fellow travelers, mostly fur-trade officials and explorers, to help us know the voyageur.

What *does* the beauty of the north country give to those who interact with it? Those who visit and travel by foot, canoe, or kayak through today's protected wilderness areas —the Boundary Waters, Quetico, Isle Royale, the wild shores of Lake Superior—can answer that for themselves.

To recall the human heritage of wild regions does not diminish their value as wilderness. Honoring the past increases the wealth of experience we share, and should protect, as responsible, caring members of the natural world we live in.

I hope this book encourages you to explore the heritage of these regions in greater depth. More about the research and process involved in creating these paintings, with suggested further readings, is given in the Afterword and Further Resources at the end of this book.

Howard Sivertson
Grand Marais, Minnesota

The Annual Cycle

The demands of European fashion, coupled with the desire of North American Indians to trade for merchandise useful to them, created a continental enterprise that, for some decades in the late 1700s, flowed in great measure through a small outpost on the western end of Lake Superior called Grand Portage.

Europeans prized the lush furs from northern otter, lynx, marten, and especially beaver. The pelts were used to make clothing accessories like hand-muffs and, shredded and formed into lustrous felt, to make men's hats—from the tri-cornered hats of the late 1700s to the stovepipe top-hats of the 1800s.

For their part, North American Indians wanted the iron tools, wool blankets, colorful cloth, guns, and other goods offered for their furs. Enthusiastic trading began in the early 16th century between European cod fishermen and the Micmac Indians of the east coast.

By the mid-1700s, French explorers had pushed the trading network well over 1,000 miles into the western Great Lakes and beyond.

French control of this network ended in 1763 (after the Seven Years' War) when France ceded Canada to the English. Thereafter, two rival companies grew to dominate the North American fur trade. The English-owned Hudson's Bay Company (est. 1670) already owned a trading monopoly for the watershed of Hudson Bay, a vast territory with relatively easy access to the sea.

In competition, a group of independent traders using the Great Lakes network formed their own confederacy. Led by Scottish-born businessmen, this group of shareholders officially organized in 1784 as the powerful North West Company.

Headquartered in Montreal, the North West Company reached across the Great Lakes. Following inland rivers and chains of smaller lakes, the Northwesters penetrated far into the northern plains and beyond, to distant Lake Athabaska and the Mackenzie, Liard, and Peace rivers.

Providing the labor to move mountains of furs and barter goods along this great trade route of over 3,000 miles were the legendary canoemen, the *voyageurs*. With vast distances of wilderness to cover, the North West Company needed men who could travel far, work tirelessly, and live simply. Stocky, powerful men, the voyageurs could paddle briskly for long hours with little rest. They could carry goods and furs in 180-pound loads over portages. They could subsist for months on pea soup, corn mush or buffalo *pemmican*—all for low wages and near-indentured service to the company.

Most of the voyageurs were French-Canadians. There were also sizeable numbers of *métis* (mixed-blood descendants of European traders and Indian wives or mistresses). Some Indians and other nationalities were also represented in the voyageur brigades.

While the shareholders and clerks of the North West Company tended to have names like McLeod, McTavish, Macdonell, and Mackenzie, their employees typically had names like La Roy, Cadieu, Ducharm, and Le Fevre. When it came to asking a blessing before running a foaming rapids, cursing when shouldering a heavy pack, or vociferously singing a bawdy paddling song... the language generally was French-Canadian.

The linchpin of the North West Company was the Grand Portage post, located midway between the far northwest and Montreal. There, at this central depot, the voyageur brigades of the company met each July to exchange cargoes.

It was a bold concept involving a lot of financial risk, yet with tremendous fortunes to be made. Each year, the shareholders shipped trade goods from Montreal to Grand Portage in large 36-foot birchbark canoes. At the same time, furs collected the previous winter at the inland posts were sent out in smaller 25-foot canoes to the *rendezvous* site. At Grand Portage, the men exchanged their cargoes—furs for trade goods—then hurried back to their home bases before winter came.

For a few weeks each midsummer, more than 1,000 canoemen gathered from across the continent. The company partners held their annual business meeeting, and everyone from the gentlemen down to the lowly voyageur feasted, danced, imbibed, and celebrated intensely. After rendezvous, the brigades headed home and the post employees settled down to a quieter life.

This painting gives an overview of the annual cycle of the North West Company in 1792. Clockwise from the top left, the painting shows a canoe from the interior approaching the inland end of the Grand Portage trail. Next, voyageurs carry 90-pound packs of furs, two at a time, across the grueling 8.5-mile portage to the stockade where the rendezvous is well under way. While company partners meet in the Great Hall, a large Montreal canoe arrives on the lake with the sloop *Athabaska*. At the bottom is a view of the stockade from a nearby Indian encampment. Finally, the cycle begins again as wintering traders bargain with their Indian neighbors for another crop of animal pelts.

In 1803, the North West Company abandoned their Grand Portage trading post to move north across the Canadian border, to build a new post, Fort William. In 1821, the North West Company merged with its arch-rival, the Hudson's Bay Company. After that, most furs from the interior were transported over easier routes to Hudson Bay.

Hivernant's Departure

Each year in May, when the ice on lakes turned black and rivers began to flow, the *hivernants* (winterers) of the north grew restless. Soon, the time came to leave their inland trading posts. With bundles of valuable furs packed tightly, canoes were launched in icy waters. Bows were pointed toward the midsummer rendezvous, and with a few quick strokes, the first northern brigades were underway.

The *hivernants* were voyageurs, company clerks, and managing partners stationed at trading posts in the *pays d'en haut* (the "Upper Country" or great interior of the continent). The wintering employees included experienced voyageurs engaged by the company year-round, often for a two- or three-year contract.

These back-country voyageurs seldom hesitated to point out that they were a class of canoemen far superior to the part-time voyageurs engaged each spring in Montreal, the so-called *mangeurs de lard* or "pork-eaters."

Many of the *hivernants* were family men who married Indian women and raised children of mixed blood (*métis*). A native wife provided companionship and household assistance for the wintering voyageur. She also provided valuable trading and social connections with her relatives in the neighboring Indian tribes.

Winters were spent trading with the Indians, fishing, and hunting buffalo, moose, and other wild game. At the post, the voyageurs built and repaired canoes, sledges, and kegs. They chopped and hauled firewood. They cut and squared logs for buildings. By dog team, the men traveled to and from Indian camps, with toboggans and sledges loaded with goods to barter. They returned with piles of cured furs, quantities of dried and fresh meat, and bladders of animal grease prepared by the native families.

When spring break-up was imminent, the men took the pelts collected from the Indians and pressed the furs into tightly-bound 90-pound packs. These heavy bales were carefully marked with their contents and stored in a warehouse until the thick ice on lakes and rivers rotted and disappeared, allowing canoes to begin their long journey to rendezvous.

The bales of furs were loaded into North canoes with provisions and other supplies. A North canoe was typically about 25 feet long. Manned by five or six voyageurs, each canoe could carry more than a ton of furs, food, and gear.

As was common when men leave families behind on their way to high adventure, farewells were said with mixed emotions. On one hand, it would be months before they saw their families again. On the other hand, the long, cold winter of isolation and, sometimes, near-starvation was over. Spring and rebirth were just over the horizon to the east and south... toward Grand Portage.

Only two months and up to 2,000 miles of canoeing across half of the continent—paddling sometimes for sixteen or eighteen hours a day, carrying their heavy cargoes over countless portages—separated the winterers from the regale of rendezvous.

H. SIVERTSON
©1987

H. SIVERTSON
©1987

Rubbaboo

For the Montreal voyageurs of the east, their diet consisted of corn mush, pea soup, and pork fat. But it was the buffalo that fed the voyageurs of the Canadian interior.

Fur-trade posts located on the northern plains, such as those on the North and South branches of the Saskatchewan River, harvested wandering herds of buffalo to stockpile food for the spring voyages. Indian, *métis*, or French-Canadian hunters brought in huge quantities of buffalo meat from which tons of *pemmican* were processed.

Pemmican was a dense, energy-rich mix which the Indians had developed as a portable, lasting food suitable for long travels. Buffalo meat—or sometimes moose or caribou—was dried, then pounded to a fine texture. The powdered meat was mixed with lard rendered from the animal's fat. Sometimes, dried berries were added for extra nutrition.

Pemmican could be stored without refrigeration for many months. Its high nutritional value, lasting qualities, and easy preparation made pemmican the perfect food for energy-burning voyageurs.

For canoe travels, the dense mass was packed into buffalo-hide sacks, each weighing 90 pounds. The bags were relayed to posts located on central waterways to resupply passing canoe brigades en route from distant posts. Four such sacks, loaded in a canoe, would get the *hivernants* about 500 miles—from one pemmican supply post to the next.

On their spring voyage to rendezvous, the Northmen ate only two meals a day... generally both of pemmican. Imagine paddling for six to eight weeks, covering a thousand miles or more, on such a diet. The men broke camp each morning before daybreak and paddled until sunrise, when they first stopped for breakfast... perhaps on a small island like this one. After a simple meal of boiled pemmican, followed by a pipe of tobacco, they resumed paddling.

Underway, the men were reported to keep a brisk pace, up to 40 to 60 paddle-strokes per minute—nearly a stroke per second! Traveling at that speed, they burned a lot of calories in an eighteen-hour day.

For the men from the farthest posts, it was a race to get to Grand Portage. There, for a few weeks, they worked, rested, and celebrated. Then, they sped homeward again. The *hivernants* feared an early freeze-up of northern lakes and rivers. Given the short summers of the north, a round trip of up to four months of travel allowed little time to rest along the way.

The second meal of the day came only at sunset, when they stopped to camp and "enjoy" another meal of pemmican.

To vary the monotonous diet, a thick soup called "rubbaboo" was sometimes made... from pemmican, of course. A mixture of flour and water, seasoned with a little maple sugar, was brought to a boil in a large kettle hung on a tripod over a fire. Chunks of pemmican were chopped off the dense hunk in a sack, added to the hot slurry, then stirred to a thick porridge-like consistency.

The voyageurs sometimes seated themselves around the large pot, each one eating from the same pot with a spoon or ladle. If in a hurry, they might pour the soup on a depression in a rock to let it cool faster, then lap it up like a dog. Sometimes they ate from their own cup or dish, but almost any container served a hungry voyageur well in an emergency. They were known to fill a handkerchief—or even a hat—and eat directly from that.

Running the Rapids

The *bourgeois* (gentleman) in charge of a northern trading district depended on the safe handling of each canoe under his supervision. The loss of cargo from even one canoe, laden with furs going to Grand Portage or trade goods on the return journey, could mean great financial loss.

For the voyageur, not only his job but his very life depended on the handling of his canoe, in and out of the water. The fragile nature of a bark canoe demanded careful treatment.

To build a bark canoe, a rough mold was made in the shape of a canoe by pounding stakes into the ground. Large sheets of birchbark were sewn together with *watap* (split spruce root), shaped, and laced to flexible gunwale strips and over stern and bow stems. Ribs of white cedar were cut, bent to shape by steaming, and inserted into the canoe's inside. Extra boards of thin cedar were then slipped in between the ribs and bark for structural support.

To prevent water from leaking in, all the sewn seams were covered with pitch that was boiled and mixed with tallow and charcoal. Poles were laid lengthwise on the inside of the canoe bottom, and the cargo packs were piled on those.

Minor breaks in the bark while traveling could be repaired with a kit of spare materials carried in each canoe, consisting of rolls of bark and spruce root and a kettle of pitch. A common evening chore of the voyageurs, by the light of a campfire, was to boil pitch and reapply it to leaky seams. En route, a large sponge was used to bail out water.

The light construction of the birchbark canoe made it easy to *portage* (carry overland). To portage from one lake to another, or to go around a dangerous stretch of rapids, the bundles of cargo were all lifted out of the canoe just offshore. The men would carry the packs and canoe over a well-worn trail through the woods to the next navigable stretch of water.

Other procedures on rivers consisted of unloading part or all of the packs and passengers so the canoe, empty or only partially laden, could be taken through the water obstacle. The lightened canoe might be paddled, poled, or towed by lines upstream, or several voyageurs would ride the canoe downstream through rapids or rocky shallows.

Running a wild rapids was a risky procedure. It saved time and energy—if all went well. The men had to judge the risk based on the amount of water flowing down the river. A rapids safe in one season could be deadly in another. High water caused a faster current, while low water exposed more dangerous rocks.

Running a rapids could be a wild, exhilerating descent. The canoemen steered their fragile vessel around rocks, through boiling eddies, and over sudden drops. A slight miscue could destroy a canoe or cause damage forcing the whole brigade to stop for repairs. The voyageurs were more apt to take this chance if no company officials were present.

A single mistake could end their lives as well. Crosses were erected at treacherous rapids in memory of foolhardy men who risked their lives, and lost.

H. SIVERTSON
©1987

H. SIVERTSON
©1988

The Pipe

The length of a long portage trail was measured in *poses*, or resting places. These were spaced about one-third to one-half mile apart, depending on the difficulty of the terrain. Packs were carried to the first *pose* and deposited, then the men went back for the remaining loads. When all the packs were at the first *pose*, the pieces were shuttled on to the next resting spot, and so on until the end of the portage was reached. This method kept the packs more or less together on a long trail, and gave the men many short walking breaks as they went back for the next heavy load.

At the end, the pieces were loaded back into the canoes, which had been portaged overland or run through a rapids to arrive well before the several tons of burdensome goods or furs showed up.

Regardless of the contents, each pack was generally made into a standard bundle weighing 90 pounds. It was common for a voyageur to carry two 90-pound packs at a time. Borrowing again from Indian methods, the voyageurs employed a system which used a "tump-line," a long leather strap of moose-hide which passed around the top of the man's forehead. This helped him lift and steady a pack halfway up his back. A second pack was often balanced on top of the first, and off he went—often at a trot—to the first pose.

On the water, distance was measured by a different method: in "pipes," or resting times. The voyageurs might paddle from 45 minutes to two hours at a stretch, until the guide's command of "*allumez*" ("light up!") was given. The paddles were immediately laid down and clay pipes were quickly filled with tobacco and lit. The canoemen smoked, chatted, and relaxed for ten to fifteen minutes before resuming paddling.

The time between pipes could vary, as did the distance, depending on paddling conditions. Traveling upstream or down, with or against the wind affected how many miles were covered and how soon the men would need to rest again.

In spite of the inaccuracy of the "pipe" system of measurement, it worked for the voyageurs. The men understood the effort involved in crossing a big "five-pipe lake." Factoring in the day's variables of wind and flow of water, they could come up with a good idea of what they were facing.

Often pipes were taken on the water, the men letting the canoe drift lazily during the rest. In the middle of a lake, there were fewer bugs to bother the men. But in some situations it was almost impossible to stop and rest on the water. A strong headwind would blow the heavily-laden canoe backward if paddling stopped. Such rests would be cut short if taken at all.

Likewise, on shore, if mosquitoes and black flies were bad, the voyageurs would not stop to rest and be devoured by the bugs. I've been on canoe trips where, after struggling for hours on a big lake against a headwind, we landed at a portage only to be attacked by swarms of mosquitoes and black flies. We would rush across the portage and shove off into the wind again, with no opportunity to rest.

The best solution on such a day was to tie up to a small island well out into a lake. Here, strong winds helped to scour the little island free of bugs. I'm sure the voyageurs sought relief in the same fashion.

Souffle, Souffle la Vieille!

Imagine you are a French-Canadian voyageur, arriving at yet another portage after paddling your North canoe for hours against a strong headwind. It's a hot day. The mosquitoes and black flies swarm to attack you the moment you land and start to unload the canoe.

No time to rest now! You load two 90-pound packs on your back and jog over the portage, trying to escape the insects that cover your skin and are inhaled as you gasp for breath. You have to make several torturous trips, back and forth, to get all the packs and canoe to the next lake. There, you hastily load your canoe and start paddling again in search of relief.

Then, as your aching, overheated, exhausted body swings into the rhythm of paddling down a long stretch of water... the wind changes direction to blow directly from astern! A cheer goes up from the crew. A short mast is quickly set up and a blanket or oilcloth sail is rigged. The canoe surges forward as the wind fills the sail, pushing you on a free ride down a long expanse of lake.

In unison, the voyageurs shout, *"Souffle, souffle, la vieille!" Blow, blow, old woman of the wind!* The men scatter tobacco on the lake and sprinkle water from canoe paddles in an old tradition of respect borrowed from the Indians.

With the wind at your back, you light your pipe and enjoy the relief from pain. This is the euphoria that comes only to those who earn it. There is time for singing, story-telling, or just smoking and watching ravens and seagulls soaring overhead among the scudding clouds.

Most canoes on long trips carried a small mast and sail to take advantage of a wind that blew directly astern. Because the voyageur canoe had a flat bottom, with no keel or centerboard, only a wind coming directly from behind made sailing possible.

On a strenuous journey like that of the voyageurs, pushing physical endurance to the limit, happiness can come quickly on the heels of pain. As pain leaves, a feeling of well-being moves in to fill the void. With swift transformation, jubilance breaks forth, the high spirits of sore muscles suddenly at ease.

Sailing with the wind at his back was about as good as a voyageur could feel—without suffering a hangover later.

H. SIVERTSON
©1987

H. SIVERTSON

Brigade from Montreal

While the winterers were preparing to journey from the interior toward Grand Portage, the eastern brigades were assembling at a place called Lachine, on the St. Lawrence River just upstream from Montreal. Large cargo canoes were being loaded with trade goods to resupply the trading posts of the northwest for another winter. Like the Northmen, the Montreal brigades gathered their crews in early May and prepared to embark for rendezvous.

The voyageurs of the North West Company were mostly French-Canadians, with *métis*, Indians, and other nationalities represented. Some were seasoned veterans. Many of the new *engagés* were drawn from the towns and farms around Montreal. Muscular fellows, the recruits were chosen for their strength and for compactness. The typical voyageur was short, probably under five and one-half feet tall, and weighed 140 to 150 pounds. A good singing voice was also considered a useful skill.

The large Montreal canoes were 36 to 40 feet long—about a dozen feet longer than a typical North canoe—and six feet wide in the middle. Each of these big canoes was capable of carrying about 60 packs—over 5,000 pounds of cargo, or twice the load of a North canoe—plus a crew of perhaps eight or ten men. Yet the empty canoe was light enough to be carried by four to six men over portages.

The canoes were swift on rivers and flexible enough to ride moderate waves on the Great Lakes. The fragile craft were frequently damaged but easily repaired with birchbark, cedar, pitch, and spruce roots.

Most importantly, with fortunes at stake, the speedy canoes were able to keep to the tight schedule needed to get trading goods to rendezvous and furs back to Montreal on time. In comparison, the early sailing ships of the fur trade, like the sloop *Athabaska*, were slow and undependable.

Not until the mid-1850s, when a lock installed at Sault Ste. Marie allowed sailing vessels and steamships to pass between Lake Huron and Superior, did transportation by ship become more effective. Until then, most fur-trade cargo traveled in bark canoes, propelled by bands of strong-armed voyageurs singing *chansons* to the rhythm of their dipping paddles.

From Montreal, their course headed west up the Ottawa River, and up the Mattawa to cross Lake Nipissing. They journeyed down the French River to Georgian Bay. The North Channel of Lake Huron led them towards Sault Ste. Marie (the rapids of the St. Mary's River) which connected Lakes Huron and Superior.

The brigades halted first at Mackinac, then at the Sault where the North West Company had a sawmill, a farm, and warehouses. Eventually, the company built a small canal allowing canoes to bypass the rapids. Taking on needed provisions, the brigades were ready for the last leg of the journey.

Arriving on Lake Superior, the canoes followed the east and north shores around to Grand Portage, arriving by early July. The 1,200-mile voyage by canoe from Montreal took from six to eight weeks.

Paddling along the base of gigantic rock palisades, past beaches of sand and cobblestone, threading their way through offshore islands and across large inlets, the voyageurs were surrounded by some of the most spectacularly beautiful scenery in North America.

Caught in a Northeaster

The trip along Lake Superior was perhaps the most dangerous portion of the journey. The voyageurs paddled briskly, their canoes hugging the shoreline for protection from the lake's unpredictable storms and confusing fog. If a sudden storm caught the brigade in open water, the canoes, men, and cargo were in extreme danger. In very heavy seas, the thin-skinned canoes could break up if not handled expertly, with a sure loss of life in the icy-cold water.

The men hurried along with the utmost speed. Full appreciation of the gorgeous scenery passing by in slow motion may have been difficult for the voyageurs and passengers, plagued by the nagging fear of disaster. Even on dead-calm days, they knew the weather could only get worse. Lake Superior's sudden storms were notorious.

The brigade followed close to the shoreline whenever possible, even when it meant paddling more miles. In some places, the canoes were protected by strings of offshore islands. In other portions of the route, the canoes had to pass by long stretches of rocky headlands rising hundreds of feet above the waters, with no safe harbors.

Elsewhere the shoreline was cut by long, deep inlets. Crossing a big bay or inlet—some of which were twenty miles wide—by heading straight across was a risk taken only after some deliberation and prayer.

If caught in a big storm, finding immediate shelter was a matter of life and death. Sometimes, the brigade had no choice but to weather through as best it could, while searching for a safe harbor or at least an island behind which to hide.

In the book *Five Fur Traders of the Northwest*, a company clerk, John Macdonell, describes his first trip in a Montreal canoe to Grand Portage in 1793. They traveled the entire Lake Superior portion of the voyage, a leg of over 400 miles, in about six days, including one day forced ashore by bad weather.

On his first journey into the western regions, young Macdonell, only twenty-five years old, did a decent job of recording many items of interest about the voyageurs and their travels and customs. Still, one wishes that Macdonell was a little less bookkeeper and a little more poet in his descriptions. The brevity and understatement common in most of the diaries and journals of the day tell more about the stoic, business-like nature of fur-trade officials than about the experience of traveling a thousand miles with the voyageurs through the wilderness in a canoe.

In the few phrases penned as a single day's entry in a clerk's journal, an imaginative writer could easily find enough material for several good short stories, at least.

H. SIVERTSON
©1986

Dégradé

Caught by a big storm, the brigade had little choice but to seek shelter and wait it out. The voyageurs called this condition *dégradé*—being forced ashore, having to wait for the weather to clear.

Despite the dangers of the storm, a voyageur's pride suffered some loss of dignity, giving in to nature's forces and having temporarily to abandon the journey. Yet I am sure that all the men in the brigade felt a little better when they saw the leading canoe head for shore and shelter. One by one, the heavily-laden canoes entered the welcome protection of a small cove.

It must have taken a few moments for the customary bluster of the men to return. First, freed from a life-and-death struggle against powerful winds and waves, the voyageurs felt an overwhelming sense of relief.

In the protected cove or bay, damaged canoes were hauled out of the water so that split seams could be repaired. Water was bailed out of other canoes, and wet packs of goods carried to land.

If forced to land on a rocky harbor on Lake Superior, unloading could be a tricky task. Rather than risk unloading heavy packs from canoes being tossed about by a surging sea, with jagged rocks lurking just below the surface, I suspect that a different process may have taken place.

It is possible the canoes were left in the water, sterns anchored, bows tied to shore. Leaving enough slack in the lines would allow the canoes to "work" up and down in the seas while keeping their hulls safe from rocks.

When the weather cleared a little, wet goods were unpacked and spread on rocks and bushes to dry. Perhaps a song would be struck up by an old hand. Gradually, the nerves of new recruits calmed as they realized they had just weathered their first big storm.

A few hours or a whole day spent in *dégradé* allowed time for hunting and berry picking, pipe smoking, and relaxation. The evening's meal and campfire was prepared earlier than usual, giving the veteran voyageurs plenty of opportunity to tease the novices with tales of exploits and conquests from previous rendezvous.

When the storm passed and waves settled, the canoes were loaded and the brigade was underway once again, bows pointed towards Grand Portage, whose distance could now be measured —weather permitting—in just days.

Lifting Fog

Although much of Lake Superior's North Shore consists of large escarpments, palisades, huge boulders, and rocky shores, the voyageurs found the occasional beach of sand or small pebbles. These spots made excellent campsites. In a cove protected from the wind and waves, a beach also provided the best place to haul out and launch canoes.

There is very little description of the usual procedure for overnight camping on Lake Superior's shores. In a painting by Frances Anne Hopkins, "Voyageurs at Dawn," the artist—who traveled in the 1860s with the voyageurs on several long trips —depicted the men camping on a beach of boulders and cobblestones, sleeping under their canoes.

A cobblestone beach may have been unavoidable on occasion, or in an emergency, but I am sure the voyageurs would have greatly favored a sand or pebble beach. A night spent lying on large cobblestones, without any type of mattress, would have been uncomfortable even for the toughest voyageur.

A rocky beach also meant large moss-covered rocks lying just under water offshore. This made loading and unloading heavy pieces of cargo in and out of canoes a slippery, precarious operation to be avoided if possible.

Unloading on a sand or pebble beach was much safer. The canoes could be paddled close to shore. The men would jump into the water and carry the 90-pound packs ashore to stack them well back from the water's edge. The voyageurs would then lift each canoe from the water and walk ashore with it.

The large canoes made decent overnight shelters. Gently placed at an upside-down angle on the sand, the canoe was rested on one edge, braced by the bow and stern tips which kept the canoe from rolling. The shelter was completed by propping canoe paddles along the open edge to support a few blankets hung over the open side. The birchbark canoe was transformed from a means of transportation to a voyageur's home away from home.

Morning fog is common on Lake Superior. If too thick, the mist could delay the regular schedule of launching in the predawn hours. Breaking camp would be postponed until the fog lifted enough so the guides could see navigational obstructions and landmarks.

When the fog diminished a little, the canoes were lifted off the beach and set in the water. Held in position by two voyageurs, the bark canoes were carefully loaded. If company officials were not up and ready to go, the voyageurs gleefully had a good excuse to pull the tents down with the gentlemen inside.

Carrying 90-pound packs across beaches with loose sand could be tiring. I suspect the voyageurs would sometimes form a chain and pass the packs from man to man, out to the waiting canoes. The men packing the canoes would arrange all the pieces tightly into the canoe interiors, leaving just enough room for the paddlers and passengers to take their places.

Soon the brigade was out on the open waters again, the men refreshed and ready for another day's journey.

H. SIVERTSON
©1987

H. SIVERTSON
©1987

Gull Eggs

Pea soup and pork, corn mush (hominy) and grease, and pemmican were the energy-packed staples that fueled the voyageurs of the North West Company. The "pork-eaters" got their nickname from the fairly decent pea-soup-and-salt-pork mixture they started with on the first leg of their journey from Montreal.

At Sault Ste. Marie, they took on new provisions, the diet switching to corn mush enriched with lard or bear grease. This plainer food sustained them on the final leg of their trip around the North Shore of Lake Superior to Grand Portage—and most of the way back to Montreal again.

Whatever staple was in the canoes, the men ate it twice a day, each and every day, for weeks on end. The standard ration, whether pemmican or pea soup, was about one quart per day. Only rarely did the voyageurs have an opportunity to break the monotony, supplementing their diet with food found along the way.

In the spring, seagull eggs were stolen from nests found on offshore islands along the canoe route. The eggs were eaten raw or cooked. One favorite recipe was a *galette*, or bread, made by mixing eggs with flour, then frying the dough in a pan, similar to the bannock of the Scottish.

If chanced upon, fresh meat from fish, ducks, turtles, or muskrat could give occasional respite from the standard fare. A stew of venison, bear, or caribou meat would be a delicacy after a few weeks of nonstop rubbaboo or pea soup. Sometimes passing Indian families could be convinced to sell or trade wild game or fish to the canoemen.

In general, however, unless they were in *dégradé* with time on their hands, the brigades were on too tight a schedule to organize a hunt or spend time fishing. Any game had to present itself to the voyageurs handily to be harvested without any loss of time.

Small treats plucked along the way included blueberries, raspberries, thimbleberries and gooseberries, growing in thickets and meadows near camps or along the portage trails.

The *hivernants*, especially, hurrying to and from distant posts in the northwest, needed to avoid being caught by an early freeze-up. They had the least time to seek culinary opportunities en route. If their rations ran out, they pressed on, hoping to find Indian camps along the route where they could barter for food.

Despite the lack of variety, the endless kettles of rubbaboo, pea soup, or corn mush and grease provided nearly all the calories the men needed to paddle and carry heavy loads all day—and still have energy left for evening pleasures... like sitting around a campfire to gum a leaky canoe seam.

Montreal Express

The 36-foot *canot de maître*, or Montreal canoe, was the primary carrier of trade goods and furs between Montreal and Grand Portage. When time deadlines were flexible, the North West Company shipped some loads of heavy, bulky freight across Lake Superior from the Sault to Grand Portage on the 45-ton sloop *Athabaska* and the 75-ton schooner *Otter*.

Where extra speed was necessary, fur-trade accounts often mention the *canot leger*, the light or express canoe. An express canoe was used for missions involving high-ranking company partners, government officials, or urgent mail.

Some light canoes were specially designed for speed. The bottom was narrower, offering less resistance in the water when lightly loaded. Besides the sleeker hull, extra paddlers could be added to push the canoe even faster. A specially-made express canoe was a prestige item, reflecting on the importance of the owner. Naturally, such a canoe was often more handsomely painted than a bulky freight canoe.

Other times, a light canoe was merely a trade canoe lightly burdened. In an emergency, a brigade could create an express canoe from a freight canoe simply by redistributing the packs from that canoe to the rest of the brigade. With a few extra voyageurs borrowed from other crews to increase paddle-power, the lightened canoe could be speeding on its way with an urgent message or important dignitary in a matter of minutes.

The oil painting illustrates an express canoe from Montreal carrying important passengers and mail to Grand Portage on a beautiful day during midsummer. They glide past Pigeon Point, not far from the protected harbor where the Grand Portage post is located.

Of all the landmarks on the traditional canoe route—many, like the Sleeping Giant of Thunder Bay, still familiar to today's travelers—none were more welcome to the voyageurs than those near Grand Portage which heralded the end of a long trip.

The beautiful scenery and placid water come as a welcome sight, concluding safely a canoe journey on ever-unpredictable Lake Superior.

H. SIVERTSON
©1989

H. SIVERTSON
©1988

Brigade in the Fog

The dense fogs of Lake Superior were less a danger and more a nuisance to the voyageur brigades hugging the North Shore en route to Grand Portage in late June. Lake fog is caused when the warmer air from the land meets cool, moist air over the lake. With very deep, cold waters, Lake Superior is especially prone to fog.

In foggy conditions, often the winds were fairly calm. Still, a befogged brigade suffered from a certain amount of confusion. There was potential danger in not picking the right course through the many islands and rocky reefs scattered in their path. The same islands and reefs that offered protection from stormy winds and seas were now obstacles to be avoided.

A brigade could include as many as thirty canoes, but a typical brigade was made up of four to eight canoes. Each brigade employed a head guide, a man specially engaged for his knowledge of the long, winding route. As well, each Montreal canoe had an experienced voyageur, the *avant*, positioned in the bow. This bowsman relayed instructions to the steersman, or *gouvernail*, who stood in the stern with a long paddle. These two members of the crew were often paid more than the others.

Most of the propulsion was provided by six to eight middlemen, or *milieux*. Sitting in the middle of the canoe, these men typically paddled 40 to 60 fairly short, powerful strokes per minute, up to eighteen hours a day. Their only breaks from paddling came at breakfast, during the periodic "pipe" rest, and, on rivers, for portages—when the work changed to heavy lifting to move 5,000 pounds of cargo overland.

I suspect the confusion created by dense fog caused many animated discussions between the brigade guide and the *avants* of the following canoes. Opinions could vary greatly as to where they were and in which direction to proceed.

The brigade's course was set by the head guide. In heavy fog, though, each voyageur could imagine he saw the faint outline of land almost anywhere he looked. I am sure there was much grumbling in the ranks as the brigade guide set his course according to his own sense of direction and mental map.

If the fog was not too thick, the voyageurs tried to follow the vague outline of the slightly darker shoreline. But dense fog might force the brigade to tie up to land and wait for the fog to lift.

Navigating in a fog requires all the senses. The sound of seagulls and shorebirds' calls, or waves breaking on rocks and beaches, combined with the smells of trees, wild flowers, and guano to indicate the whereabouts of land to an experienced voyageur... even when his eyes had nothing to see.

Sprucing Up

North West Company clerk, John Macdonell, passed through Grand Portage en route to his first wintering post on the river Qu' Appelle, a tributary of the Assiniboine. In his diary of 1793 he records his canoe's approach to Grand Portage from Montreal:

"[July 7] ...Leaving pointe au père we paddled two pipes and put to shore to give the men time to clean themselves, while we breakfasted—this done a short pipe brought us to *Pointe au Chapeaux* around which we got a sight of the long wished for Grand Portage."

Other travelers during the North West Company's regime reported the same custom of stopping to clean up before their grand entrance into Grand Portage. The voyageurs were proud, dressy fellows. Some were even described as dandies when attired in their fineries.

The last few miles of the canoe route to Grand Portage took voyageurs through the Suzie Islands, just a short paddle from Pointe aux Chapeaux. There are several islands with sand and pebble beaches that offer easy access and protection from the winds. For my painting, I chose a small island with a spit of sand beach located on the west end of the Suzie archipelago.

A sense of excitement would be in the air, especially for the youngest men from Montreal on their first trip. After the 1,200-mile journey, they now anticipated paddling around the next point to the fantasy land of rendezvous. Obviously, they wanted to look their best when rounding the point.

Hair was trimmed, then the men scrubbed up in the cold waters that quickened heartbeats even more. Personal packs were pulled from under canoe seats where they had been stored. Out came the best of the men's shirts, woven sashes, scarves, and jaunty caps.

I imagine after donning their brightly-colored shirts, sashes, and ostrich plumes, they strutted about a bit while doing their final preening. The canoes were also festooned with brigade and company flags. If dignitaries were aboard, the Union Jack was unfurled.

I only presume the men might have pressed their leaders to open a keg of high wine or rum to toast the upcoming event, adding still more excitement to the festive air. Refreshed and cleaner, the men climbed back in their canoes and pushed off.

Maybe some of their naughtiest, liveliest *chansons* were sung to set a quick-paddle tempo as they rounded Pointe aux Chapeaux. Digging a little deeper and pulling a little harder with each paddle stroke, the men would summon their finest voices in song to answer the gun salutes that rang forth from the stockade when the approach of the brigade was spotted. Throngs of voyageurs already at rendezvous would gather on the shore to cheer the arrival of this newest contingent.

H. SIVERTSON

H. SIVERTSON
©1987

Rounding Hat Point

The goal of the 1,200-mile journey from Montreal came into view as the brigade rounded Pointe aux Chapeaux, or Hat Point. With renewed energy from their brief stop in the Suzie Islands to get dressed up, the powerful canoemen set a spirited pace. Paddles kept time to a rhythmic *chanson*. A salute from the cannon and a volley of musket fire from the stockade at the bottom of the harbor heralded the voyageurs' grand entrance.

It was a time of great excitement, especially for the young Montrealers making their first journey to rendezvous. Many were young lads from farms around the St. Lawrence River, away from the demands of family and priests for the first time. It was not visions of sugar plums that danced through their heads but the promise of exotic fantasies soon to be fulfilled. The images had been planted in the minds of new recruits by the veteran voyageurs, whose heroic tales of exploits at past rendezvous had gained embellishment with each telling.

But the celebration did not start immediately. In his contract, each "pork-eater" had agreed to make a specified number of carrying trips—typically three or four—over the rugged 8.5-mile Grand Portage. This trail ran through the hills behind the Grand Portage post, north and west to Fort Charlotte on the Pigeon River. The eyes of the newcomers could not help but be drawn, with some misgivings, to the hills looming behind the stockade.

On each trip over the portage trail, the Montreal voyageur carried two 90-pound packs, kegs, or cases of trade goods to the banks of the Pigeon. On the way back, he carried one or two 90-pound packs of furs left at Fort Charlotte by the Northmen.

The prestigious Northmen got to leave their cargoes at Fort Charlotte to walk over the portage carrying only their personal gear—a clear sign of their higher standing with the company. Meanwhile, the Montrealers were trudging back and forth, transporting heavy packs each way, their dreams of rendezvous slightly delayed by this inconvenience.

The rivalry between the Montrealers and the winterers was the source of friction, and not a few fights, during the weeks of rendezvous. The taunts and boasts undoubtedly started as the two groups of men passed each other on the Grand Portage trail.

The powerful voyageurs were reported to make this grueling carry of 180-pound loads often at a trot, resting occasionally at *poses* spaced every one-third or one-half mile apart. Was it the promise of rendezvous that hastened those steps... or just the whine of mosquitoes?

Some of the Montrealers were selected for a special mission, to continue westward another fifteen days to Rainy Lake. There they rendezvoused with the most distant brigades of Northmen coming from Lake Athabaska. For the Athabaskans, the distance was too far and the traveling season too short to risk a round trip as far as Grand Portage. With an early freeze, two more weeks each way could have spelled disaster for them. Instead, the furs from Athabaska were exchanged for cargoes of trading goods at an inland post at Rainy Lake.

Most of the voyageurs, however, would soon be spending their time feasting, celebrating, trading yarns, renewing old friendships and making new ones. Rendezvous would certainly be a memorable time for all—even if it did not always match up fully to the wildest dreams of the young pork-eaters.

Grand Portage Stockade in 1792

Grand Portage is a geographical heart, a North American crossroads of flowing waterways. With just a few portages from the stockade, a canoe could travel to the Pacific coast, to the Arctic Ocean, to the Atlantic Ocean, or to the Gulf of Mexico. In between these distant destinations lay an entire continent—laced with rivers, linked by trading posts, settled by Native American families, and full of fur-bearing animals. Grand Portage was a little place of passing, of meeting, of moving on—and a center of great things.

The traditional portage had been used for a long time by parties of Indians, traveling to their seasonal hunting, fishing, and food-gathering spots. For generations they had held their own summer gatherings on the shores of Lake Superior to celebrate, socialize, and conduct religious ceremonies.

History records that the French explorer La Vérendrye was one of the first Europeans to use the 8.5-mile portage. In 1732 he led a group inland to Lake of the Woods where he built a trading post.

From the 1730s to the 1770s, the Grand Portage trail became a well-used gateway to a growing fur trade in the interior. By the late 1770s, a number of competing traders who used the route began to discuss a possible merger.

For two decades, 1784 to 1802, Grand Portage became the summer rendezvous point for the resulting coalition known as the North West Company. Each July, a few dozen leading traders and financiers, their clerks, and as many as 1,000 of their voyageur employees gathered in and around this stockade.

During the weeks of rendezvous, the partners conducted their annual business meeting. Meanwhile, company clerks frantically sorted, counted, credited, repacked, marked, and stored mountains of trade goods and furs.

Boxes and packs of wool blankets, bolts of cloth, beads and mirrors, cooking pots and utensils, axes and knives, guns and ammunition, animal traps, and countless other items were divided up for transport to inland posts for another year of trading with the native populations.

Furs of beaver, otter, marten, mink, fisher, ermine, wolf, deer, caribou, moose, and bear were sorted by type and quality. Detailed accounts of credits and debits were meticulously charged to the various posts and partners. The company store did a brisk business with the voyageurs, especially winterers who needed new clothes and equipment. Sales of rum and "high wines"—a type of watered-down alcohol—were also brisk to the men camping outside the stockade walls.

Inside and outside the stockade, festivities of dancing, drinking, feasting, and singing were soon underway, as the voyageurs challenged each other to games of strength, wrestling, and fighting.

Passing through in 1793, John Macdonell described the fort as having sixteen buildings, six of which were storehouses for company merchandise and furs. The rest were dwelling houses, shops, a counting house, and a mess house.

The painting shows the approximate arrangement of buildings within the stockaded walls. To the right of the stockade, the Northmen's camp was reported to be relatively orderly, in comparison to a more disheveled Montrealers' camp seen on the left. The camps were separated to maintain some level of peace between the highly competitive factions. Within each camp, the men divided themselves by brigade.

The sloop *Athabaska* lies anchored in deep water near the island, while a brigade of Montreal canoes enters the harbor to land and unload at the wharf.

H. SIVERSON

Rendezvous

Grand Portage was a hubbub of activity during the weeks of rendezvous as hundreds of voyageurs from the interior and Montreal gathered.

First, there was work to do. Furs had to be carried in from Fort Charlotte, on the far end of the 8.5-mile portage, to be inspected and repacked. Trade goods and supplies were assembled to fill various orders for the wintering posts. The packages were weighed—and marked with the weights to guard against pilfering—then carried up the portage to Fort Charlotte.

There were buildings to repair, wood to chop, canoes to mend. Most of the physical labor was done by voyageurs, the working class of the company. Not until this was accomplished could they turn to the real goal of rendezvous—in their eyes, certainly—a chance to blow off some steam.

The gentlemen of the North West Company likewise tended first to their business. They convened the annual meeting of company shareholders to plan next year's trade activities, assign new territories, and discuss personnel.

The politics were intense at times in this confederacy of traders and financiers. Shareholders vied for choice territories. Various factions formed and fought alliances. The wintering partners who ran the inland posts often saw things differently than did the suppliers and bankers of Montreal.

But it was not all work for the gentlemen, either. Play came after the business meeting was concluded. Tables were set in the Great Hall for an evening of fellowship and festivities. After a grand banquet of pork, venison, fish, fresh vegetables, potatoes, fresh bread and butter, they cleared away the tables and turned to imbibing and dancing.

Scottish bagpipes, violins, flutes, and fife issued forth jigs and reels as the gentlemen danced with the "ladies of the country"—the Indian and *métis* wives, mistresses, and daughters of the post employees—who, as one witness exclaimed, "danced not amiss."

Meanwhile the voyageurs continued their games outside the stockade walls, the gates now closed to prevent the rowdy, partisan bands of inebriated canoemen from rampaging through the grounds.

Some of the pious Christian gentlemen who observed the festivities called it debauchery. Like the gentlemen inside the Great Hall, the voyageurs drank and danced with Indian ladies around their fires. *Chansons* were sung and lively tunes played on fiddle or flute. Without the well-bred manners of the gentlemen, the voyageurs' celebration surely was a little wilder than the somewhat more reserved affair conducted inside the post.

But the consequences were the same. A hangover has the same effect no matter what your station in life.

As the evening grew long, the sounds of Scottish ballads from inside the post mingled with sentimental or humorous songs in the French-Canadian dialect outside. Drums and chants echoed from nearby Indian camps. Peals of laughter rang out over the constant murmur of hundreds of joyous celebrants.

Slowly the music of the festivities subsided. Fire embers faded. The last of the celebrants crawled away to sleep, and the chirps of frogs and crickets once again took over the night. In just a few hours the scene will be quiet, indeed, when the morning sun rises over the bay.

Sabbath Sunrise

The ebb and flow of celebration continued for six to eight weeks each summer, as newcomers arrived to refresh the mood of celebration.

The voyageurs had signed up with the company for any number of reasons. For many, it was necessity—they needed a job. Some sought escape from an unpleasant situation. Some desired the solitude of a remote wilderness, others craved the adventure that was sure to come—between the boredom and backbreaking labor.

Regardless of what lured them into months or years of low-paid service with the company, all probably saw rendezvous as a grand place to be. The young *engagés* from Montreal, who did most of the labor at rendezvous, were able to discover for themselves the truth of the adventure, romance, and the other fantasies that had drawn them westward.

For the men from the east, devout Catholics, the religious rituals of church and family back home were temporarily put on hold. For a few weeks in July, the pork-eaters were on summer break from pious clergy and parents.

For the Northmen, quite a few adopted a hybrid form of Christianity which combined French-Canadian Catholicism with Indian traditions and concepts. Many of the wintering voyageurs gradually absorbed the native beliefs of their Indian wives and families. The Indian ceremonies paid respect to local spirits—the animals, the earth, the wind. Living in an enormous natural wilderness where humans played only a small, rather insignificant role—the Indian customs made a lot of sense for those trying to survive in the *pays d'en haut*.

Even the Scottish gentlemen, meeting at rendezvous and wintering at inland posts, did not allow their Protestant upbringing to stand in their way of having a good time. Their keen practical nature and sense of adventure led them to partake of the spirit of rendezvous and the back country—while keeping a watchful eye on their investments.

The painting shows the aftermath of the preceding day's festivities. It suggests the possibility of a canoe race having been held, probably between the *hivernants* and the *mangeurs de lard*. Considering the boastful, competitive nature of the high-spirited contenders—especially after a considerable intake of rum or high wine—such a competition was inevitable.

Sober voyageurs would never have pulled their canoes onto a sand beach and left them to stay in that condition, half in the water, overnight. I presume the waking voyageurs, once their heads clear, will lift the canoes to higher ground before the *bourgeois* begin stirring about and discover the rascals' folly.

A rising sun reveals a soft fog drifting in. The peaceful countenance of the morning stands in gentle contrast to the chaotic debauchery of the evening just passed. The campfires with their games and wild abandon are only a blurred memory in the aching head of a voyageur, waiting quietly for his pot to warm up.

H. SIVERTSON
©

ATHABASKA
H. SIVERTSON
©1988

Unloading the *Athabaska*

The *bourgeois* and clerks of the fur trade were literate people who documented their business dealings in journals, diaries, and letters. Yet, despite considerable documentation of fur-trade transactions, we have little detailed information about individual voyageurs or their lives. Neither the voyageurs nor the Indian families who provided furs and expertise to the trade left written records of their experiences. Historians have had to rely mostly on surmise and conjecture, bolstered with a few brief references here and there.

Curiously, even less is known of the ships on Lake Superior used in the trade. Although sailing ships played an important role in shuttling trade goods, supplies, and furs between Lake Superior posts, I have found very little published mention of them.

We know that, between 1775 and 1780, trader John Askin operated the *De Peyster* and the *Mackinac* on Lake Superior. In 1786, the North West sloop *Athabaska* was launched, followed in 1793 by the *Otter*, then the *Invincible* and *Recovery*.

During the peak of the Lake Superior fur trade, those vessels were joined by the ships of the rival XY Company, the *Caledonia*, *Perseverance*, *Charlotte*, and *Nancy*.

The birchbark-canoe brigades, however, were still considered the most reliable way to send supplies quickly and on time. Trade goods from Montreal needed to get to Grand Portage or, after 1803, to Fort William without delay to be delivered to waiting Northmen brigades, in a hurry to travel back to their interior posts. Likewise, fur packs needed to be transported onward to Montreal in time for shipment to Europe before the St. Lawrence froze.

For the North West Company, the sloop *Athabaska* hauled items across Lake Superior that were too heavy or bulky for the canoe brigades. Sailing-ship cargoes included farm animals, cast-iron cookstoves, large barrels of flour or cornmeal, kegs of nails, and lumber. These important supplies—but generally not as crucial to the tightly-scheduled flow of business as furs and barter-goods—were shipped from the Sault on the east end of the lake to Grand Portage or Fort William on the west.

To my knowledge there is no visual documentation of the *Athabaska*, so for models I used other sloops of the same vintage, size, and mission that could be considered "sister ships." The painting shows her at anchor in Grand Portage Bay. Voyageurs are arriving to unload barrels, boxes, and crates into *bateaux* (skiffs) to row the cargo to the wharf by the stockade.

Because she was ill-designed for her mission and sailed like a tub, she was replaced in 1793 by what I believe was the schooner *Otter*. The *Athabaska* was run down the rapids of the St. Mary's River to Lake Michigan and renamed... the *Otter!*

I believe the sloop *Otter* (formerly the *Athabaska*) and her replacement on Lake Superior, the schooner *Otter*, have been confused by historians ever since.

Welcoming the *Otter*

The diary of John Macdonell, reprinted in the book *Five Fur Traders of the Northwest*, tells us what little we know about the North West Company schooner, the *Otter*.

Macdonell, a clerk, traveled with a brigade of company canoes from Montreal en route to his first post on the river Qu' Appelle, over 600 miles inland from Grand Portage. On July 2, 1793, after crossing the Sault from Lake Huron to approach Lake Superior's eastern end, they passed Pointe aux Pins, where he noted:

" —stopped at pointe au Pins where two leagues above the Sault we found Mr Nelson building a vessel for the North West Company to navigate the Lake Superior and to be called the Otter. She is to be launched shortly."

In late July, in Grand Portage, Macdonell made another entry concerning the *Otter*: "The New Ship otter has been expected some time now and we are anxiously looking out for her; provisions have turned so scarce that near 1000 men upon the ground in the company's service have been put upon half allowance. A full allowance to a voyageur while at this Poste is a Quart of Lyed Indian Corn or maize, and one ounce of Greece. It is reckoned there is only six days allowance remaining in the Stores, and should the vessel protract her arrival beyond that period I am at a loss to think what shift the gentlemen would adopt to subsist their servants."

Several days later, on August 2, 1793, Macdonell continues: "Old Bazil Ireland the guide arrived with two Montreal canoes and brings the agreeable news of the Otter lying off *Pointe au Père*. Early next morning a Boat well manned was sent to tow her up into port, and to their surprise spied her behind the point a la Framboise [Raspberry Point] after passing before the fort in the Night with a North West wind. It was ten o'clock before She anchored at the wharffe having entered partly by sailing and partly by towing."

In my painting, I tried to catch the mood of hungry voyageurs about to be saved from starvation. They surely provided a spirited welcome to sailing master John Bennet and crew of the 75-ton *Otter*, before helping to tow her into the Grand Portage bay.

After just a few years of hauling supplies to and from North West Company posts around Lake Superior, her hull rotted out. By then, the company had moved north to Fort William and built the 100-ton schooner *Invincible* to take shipments from one end of the lake to the other.

OTTER
H. SIVERTSON
©1988

H. SIVERTSON
©1988

Departing Fort Charlotte

Despite the pleasures of rendezvous, the voyageurs did not tarry long. With cargoes of fur bales inspected and repacked, the Montreal brigades left, eastbound across Lake Superior. Their canoes heavy with precious furs, the Montrealers retraced their route back along the northern and eastern shores of the big lake toward the Sault—toward the land of pea soup and salt pork.

The Northmen had already begun to disappear from rendezvous, brigade by brigade, headed for their wintering posts. Canoes from the most distant forts left first. The *hivernants* walked back over the Grand Portage to Fort Charlotte on the Pigeon River, where they had left their canoes before rendezvous. Though reluctant to leave, the voyageurs wanted to get back to their inland stations before northern waterways began to freeze in just a few months.

Named after the wife of King George III, Fort Charlotte was positioned at the inland end of the Grand Portage. Flowing past the small stockade, the Pigeon River plunged down through a series of booming, boiling cascades to its mouth on Lake Superior. Upstream, the river led westward to a long, winding chain of lakes and rivers—the canoe pathway to the interior of the continent.

There are few records documenting the physical structure of Fort Charlotte. Today only a few earthen mounds indicate where some of the buildings stood. It was briefly described by one traveler as a stockade with buildings and stores inside. We can assume the post had warehouses to store goods and furs, a canoe yard to keep North canoes safe while the *hivernants* were at rendezvous, and living quarters for the post's manager and staff.

The elite Northmen had collected their pay from the company. According to their status in the company hierarchy, this included clothing, blankets, tobacco, and other items. In the *pays d'en haut* there was little need for currency. Most transactions were recorded as credits or debits in the company books. Money could be provided to relatives in Lower Canada, if stipulated in the voyageur's contract. In the festive spirit of rendezvous, some of the winterers had signed up for another three-year engagement.

For days, they had enjoyed the camaraderie of old friends. With little cause to hold back, they had spun yarns, boasted, lied, fought, played games, and ate and drank all they could. The doctor stationed at the post had been kept very busy, treating old wounds and new.

But the meeting of the company partners was finished. Canoe cargoes of trade goods were assembled at Fort Charlotte. Rendezvous was over.

The brigades of North canoes left at two-day intervals to avoid overcrowding on the first stretches of the return route. If several brigades tried to cross a portage at the same time, in the confusion a pack could easily be picked up by the wrong brigade and transported to a distant post.

Some of the voyageurs, long-time *hivernants*, were anxious to return home to families left in the spring. But there were fresh faces in the brigades, men headed into the interior for the first time. These young clerks and promoted pork-eaters left Fort Charlotte with mixed emotions.

They could only imagine the hardships and adventures promised by new assignments in the unpredictable interior—the endless wilderness of the Great Northwest.

The Meadows

The Meadows was the first overnight campsite for the Northmen returning from rendezvous to wintering posts in the interior. Located a few miles upstream from Fort Charlotte, it was a short paddle—just enough for the men to stretch their arms a little.

At this clearing, according to one traveler, "They will have merry upon some small Kegs of Wine" which were generally given to them as a bonus upon their re-enlistment, to the tune of "one and sometimes 2 gallons to each man." A "regale" was often celebrated at this pleasant spot where the travelers found "a delightful Meadow to pitch our Tents and plenty of elbow room for the men to play their antic tricks."

The 25-foot North canoes were loaded to the gunwales with trade goods and supplies. There was hardly enough room to accommodate the five or six voyageurs, let alone the kegs of wine given to them as gifts by the company. It made good sense to get rid of some of the burdensome wine as soon as possible. This was accomplished with great efficiency at the Meadows.

The campsite was maintained by company *engagés* from Grand Portage who periodically cut or burned off the grass and brush. This held down mosquitos and black flies and presented a comfortable arena for the *hivernants*' last celebration of rendezvous.

You can be sure their departure at dawn the next morning would be relatively quiet. Once underway, heads cleared. The self-inflicted aches of last evening's festivities, on the heels of weeks of rendezvous, slowly disappeared to the healing rhythm of dipping paddles.

For any new winterers headed into the unknown for the first time, a hangover only exaggerated the anxiety and loneliness they felt. But soon, as the excitement and anticipation of high adventure worked its magic, their spirits soared again.

For some of the old hands, returning to fulfill another year of engagement, the solemn reflection might last a little longer. They knew the toll of a long winter of boredom, danger, and possible starvation. Others in the canoes, however, looked forward to returning home to wives and families.

All were united in the desire to arrive at their destination before rivers and lakes froze, causing much hardship and possibly death. A song was boldly launched. The flashing paddles held a steady rhythm, and the canoes pulled ahead with each stroke. The long journey into the continent's great interior had truly begun.

Although overgrown with alder brush, this meadow still exists. If you sit quietly and long enough... you might still hear a faint echo of "*En roulant ma boule*" or "*A la claire fontaine*." Or maybe it was just the babbling of the Pigeon River... or maybe just the wine.

H. SIVERTSON
©1987

Little Rock Portage

The *hivernants* had one more ceremony to perform as they proceeded westward from Grand Portage. Not far inland from Lake Superior, they crossed the Height-of-Land Portage. Not a difficult portage, only a 700-foot-long trail between two adjacent lakes, this was more of a symbolic crossing.

The "height-of-land" was a divide of watersheds. Before the portage, the waters drained back to Lake Superior and, through the Great Lakes and St. Lawrence River, to the Atlantic. Beyond this portage, the waters drained north to Hudson Bay.

For the voyageurs, this was the portal to the *pays d'en haut*, the Upper Country. Men who crossed this ceremonial, invisible line were due the respect of all voyageurs. In a small ritual, every novice crossing for the first time—*bourgeois*, clerk, or pork-eater—was proclaimed a "Northwester." It was decreed that henceforth each was allowed to wear a plume or feather in his cap as a sign of this elevated status.

According to the 1793 journal of the ever-observant John Macdonell, the candidate was sprinkled with a cedar branch dipped with water, then made to promise never to allow anyone to pass that way without initiation into the ranks of Nor'westers and never to kiss a voyageur's wife without her consent. A dozen gunshots were fired and a treat of high wine was expected from the new initiate.

Macdonell, a bright clerk later to become a company shareholder, had learned the ways of the voyageur well enough to suspect that the true purpose of this ceremony was to solicit the new candidate for a required gift of strong spirits. Macdonell complied and furnished a two-gallon keg from his trading stocks.

The painting shows the voyageurs on their way to a post at Rainy Lake. They are crossing the Little Rock Portage on the Granite River, just north of Gunflint Lake. Beyond Rainy Lake, the Rainy River led them to Lake of the Woods. From there, the brigades began to travel more north than west, to enter Lake Winnipeg.

Beyond that, many routes diverged. Some brigades headed west to the plains posts of the Assiniboine and Saskatchewan river systems, where much of the fur-trade's supply of buffalo pemmican was produced, as well as diverse furs collected from Indian hunters.

Others bent to their paddles and pressed far north, entering the Arctic watershed when they reached the Athabaska River, draining to distant Lake Athabaska. This was the site of a North West Company post called Fort Chipewyan. The colder climate of the Athabaskan region and, still further north, the Arctic's Mackenzie River, produced very thick, lush animal pelts much prized in European markets.

Picking Blueberries

The Montreal brigades heading home in August enjoyed the warmest and calmest time for traveling on Lake Superior. As usual, the brigades were in a hurry, with deadlines to meet. The canoes dashed along the North Shore on the first leg of their trip back towards Sault Ste. Marie, Lake Huron, and the eastern rivers leading back to Montreal.

As soon as the furs arrived in Montreal, they would be reloaded onto boats for transport down the St. Lawrence River to Quebec. Bound across the Atlantic, the furs were headed to European auction-houses. Sold to clothing designers and furriers, the pelts were crafted into the stylish felt hats and fashion accessories of the day.

Although Lake Superior was generally at its quietest in August, it could be hit by a sudden, violent storm, heralding the coming of fall with high winds and heavy seas. The homebound brigades were occasionally caught by bad weather and forced ashore to spend a few hours, or days, in *dégradé*.

Any such delay on the return trip caused great anxiety for the *bourgeois* and company clerks. They were responsible for fortunes in furs, packed in bundles, sitting on a beach in a cove in the middle of the wilderness.

It was different for the voyageurs who were thinking mostly of their stomachs. On the trip to Grand Portage, their diet had been primarily pea soup and a little pork, or corn mush. They did not fare much better at rendezvous. After an initial regale of wine or rum, fresh bread and butter, pork and fish, they had quickly been put back on a company diet of corn mush, twice a day.

They did their best to scrounge extra items from the company provisioners, from comrades, or from the Indian neighbors holding their own gatherings near the fort. Now, on their way home again, the voyageurs saw little but corn mush and grease, twice a day.

The company officials considered the hard-working voyageurs the ideal employees, to be able to subsist on such a diet. The voyageurs had their own opinion of the matter, I am sure. How often did their daydreams consist of visions of a good meal, served by a caring mother or girlfriend back home?

Homebound, the young voyageur had some time to reflect on his summer adventure. Hardened, he was looking forward to returning home where, as one fellow put it, he would have to work only like a man and not like a pack animal.

During the coming winter months, however, the pain of voyaging might be forgotten. Would memories of the good times of rendezvous rekindle the spirit of adventure? Would he become a professional voyageur, joining the canoe brigades each May as they assembled? Next time, would he sign on for a position in the interior, to become an elite *hivernant*, never again to be called a pork-eater by those haughty men of the North?

In the meantime, a brief period of rest gave the men a chance to pick the blueberries, raspberries, and thimbleberries that grew in abundance along their route home in August.

SIVERTSON
©1987

The Canoe Builders of Saganaga

If the voyageurs were the work horses of the fur trade, the Indians were its main suppliers, consumers, and trainers. The Indians befriended and taught the traders most of the skills they needed to prosper in the wilderness.

Certainly, without the support of the Indians—as hunters, pelt-curers, food-suppliers, guides, middlemen traders, and, not least, as customers interested in the barter-goods offered—the continental sweep of the fur trade would have never developed in the first place... or lasted for over 200 years.

From the first meeting of cultures, Indian guides with extensive travel and trade networks led white "explorers" to new territories, teaching them wilderness travel and survival skills. In the white-man's curious tradition, the visiting "explorers" took credit for "discovering" those lands, often claiming them for a distant king. This ignored the fact that American Indians had lived upon the lands, in harmony with its animals and plants, for thousands of years before the arrival of Europeans.

Across the continent, the native cultures were tremendously diverse. From the Micmac of the east coast to the Huron, Ottawa, Cree, and Ojibway of the Great Lakes to the Athabaskans of the northwest interior, many tribes participated in a growing partnership to swap furs for manufactured goods.

One of the most valuable native contributions to the trade was the birchbark canoe. This craft was wonderfully designed to haul heavy loads down wild rivers, through shallow marshes, and across stormy lakes. Yet it was light enough to be carried by a few men over portages, allowing long journeys through wilderness terrain.

By the late 1700s, the fur companies had their own canoe factories. The large 36-foot Montreal canoes were made by craftsmen of the North West Company at Trois Rivières near Montreal and at St. Joseph on Lake Huron. Most of the 25-foot North canoes were built by Ojibway craftsmen living near the Rainy Lake post, at Grand Portage, and, after 1803, around Fort William.

The life span of a bark canoe in the fur trade was short, lasting not much more than a season or two. The fragile bark was easily broken on submerged rocks or by frequent handling. Through constant use, canoes could become water-logged and eventually rotted. The canoes often needed to be patched and seams resealed en route, for which purpose each canoe carried a spare roll of bark, pitch, and *watap* (spruce root).

In 1800, Alexander Henry, the Younger, was headed north through Saganaga Lake, a large lake inland from Lake Superior. Needing to replace a broken canoe, he stopped at an Indian canoe-maker's camp but, his diary records, "as none of them were to my taste we proceeded to the Detroit [narrows] in the lake."

In this painting, Alexander Henry's brigade is stopping to inquire about purchasing a canoe from the Saganaga canoe builders. Oftentimes, the Indian women played a role in such negotiations as interpreters.

However, the canoe under construction is too small for a trade canoe. It is probably being built for the Ojibway family's personal use and would not serve the cargo needs of the Henry brigade.

Hunting Caribou on Isle Royale

The business of the fur trade funneled through a limited number of canoe routes and trading posts. The Indian families of the area, however, roamed more widely. Though they typically did not undertake such long routes as the professional voyageurs, the Indians used canoes for seasonal travels throughout their home districts.

The Indian cultures were highly developed to live off provisions the land offered, in good years and poor. Families picked berries and other edible or medicinal plants. They collected wild rice and produced maple sugar. They fished and hunted year-round. Over generations, they had identified the best spots to gather food during each season of the year.

On foot and by canoe, small bands traveled to and from these special places. They hunted, gathered, and processed food, storing as much as possible in small birchbark containers. The families feasted, visited, and shared what they had with relatives and neighbors, including their fur-trade partners.

Archeologists believe that Woodland Indians began to visit Isle Royale, a large island in Lake Superior just a few miles from Grand Portage Bay, as early as 2,500 B.C. These earliest visitors gathered copper, fished, and hunted. Arriving later, the Ojibway people called the island in their language "*Minong*," which means "a good place to be."

Families traveled in canoes to Isle Royale on a seasonal basis to harvest the island's rich resources. In summer, animals were hunted and berries picked. Indian fishing expeditions in the fall took advantage of Lake Superior's annual fish migration, as fish moved from deeper waters to shallow spawning reefs. Plentiful catches of fish, dried and smoked, contributed greatly to a family's winter survival.

Very few Indian families chose to winter on the island. Those who did trapped beaver, lynx, and marten for delivery to the Grand Portage post in the spring. Only winterers on the island could harvest maple syrup from island highlands in March and April. Ice fields and open water made traveling to the island in canoes or dog sleds impossible during that period.

This painting shows Indians hunting woodland caribou in Isle Royale waters in the late 1700s. Caribou were hunted summer and fall for meat and skins. The Ojibway probably used the same technique for hunting caribou herds as did Indians farther north. One group of hunters on land drove a herd into the water, toward other hunters waiting in canoes.

The men in canoes chased down the swift-swimming animals, driving their canoes right on top of the animals. A well-placed spear to the kidney killed the caribou instantly and also paralyzed it, preventing convulsions that could upset the canoe. The carcasses were then pulled to shore to be skinned and the meat divided among all the hunters.

Caribou swim much faster and float higher in the water than moose. A successful hunt required strong canoe paddlers and precise marksmanship for a hunter balanced with a spear in the bow of a surging canoe.

Caribou disappeared from Isle Royale in the 1920s. By that time too many hunters, animal predators, and incompatible moose and deer populations had encroached on their territory. There are still some woodland caribou herds in northwestern Ontario, and a small herd on Slate Island in Lake Superior.

H. SIVERTSON
©1992

H. SIVERTSON
©1992

John Tanner and the Muskegoes

The Indians left us with very little written history. Most of what we know about the native populations was written by white men and is full of inaccuracies and misinterpretations. Furthermore, two-thirds or more of the Indian populations of the northwest fur-trade regions were wiped out in a tragic 1781-82 smallpox epidemic. With disease striking down countless elder oral historians of the tribes, large gaps were left in tribal memories.

The recorded narratives of John Tanner's thirty years of "Captivity and Adventures" are a rare and fascinating account set in the late 1700s and early 1800s. A white child, Tanner was captured in Ohio and traded north to be adopted into an Ottawa family. His new mother was a female chief named Net-No-Kwa. With loving care, Net-No-Kwa raised John as her own child. Later, the family migrated to the Red River region west of Lake Superior.

John Tanner lived as an Indian until his late 30s. He later narrated his experiences to Doctor Edwin James, thereby giving us remarkable insight into the Indian cultures of the region. Young Tanner lived, hunted, trapped, and traded with posts of the North West Company and their rival, Hudson's Bay Company. Tanner's narration presents Indian viewpoints on family life, warring with the Sioux, the greed and treachery of corrupt white traders, alcohol abuse, times of starvation and abundance, and traditions of sharing among the Indians.

On several occasions, his family traveled through Grand Portage. When he was a teenager, John Tanner, his Indian brother Wa-Me-Gon-A-Biew, and mother Net-No-Kwa wintered, possibly in 1793-94, at the mouth of what they called the "burnt-wood river," the Brule River south of Grand Portage.

Earlier that winter, a band of Muskegoe Indians had found Tanner's family living in near-starvation at the Grand Portage stockade. The hospitable Muskegoes invited the hungry Ottawas to join them at their camp on the Brule for the winter. The next summer, the Muskegoes took the family to Isle Royale to hunt, fish, trap, and pick berries.

Because I was raised on Isle Royale, I was interested in this story, especially the ceremony of their departure from the island in late summer to return to the mainland. According to John Tanner:

"We were ten canoes in all, and we started, as we had done in coming, at the earliest dawn of the morning. The night had been calm, and the water, when we left the island, was perfectly smooth. We had proceeded about two hundred yards into the lake, when the canoes all stopped together, and the chief, in a very loud voice, addressed a prayer to the Great Spirit, entreating him to give us a good look to cross the lake. 'You,' said he, 'have made this lake, and you have made us, your children; you can now cause that the water shall remain smooth, while we pass over in safety.' In this manner, he continued praying for five or ten minutes; he then threw into the lake a small quantity of tobacco, in which each of the canoes followed his example. They then all started together, and the old chief commenced his song, which was a religious one..."

The Recovery Hides Out

Unlike the American frontier to the south, where pioneer settlers coveted Indian lands, the northern fur trade wanted to keep the wilderness intact to encourage Indian hunting and trading. The traders sought alliances with the Indians as trading partners, often as relatives by marriage. This allowed the voyageur canoes to travel through 3,000 miles of wilderness with little fear of attack by hostile Indians.

More dangerous to the North West Company were political intrigues from their own kind. Besides internal struggles, the company faced stiff competition from other trading companies, sometimes approaching open warfare.

Even more threatening at the end of the 18th century was a flare-up of border disputes between the United States and British Canada. Since key portions of their long route fell right along the border, the North West Company was especially vulnerable. In 1794, negotiations cast a shadow over the historic Grand Portage gateway to the interior.

To confirm lands ceded after the Revolutionary War, the Jay Treaty of 1794 named the Pigeon River as the boundary just west of Lake Superior. The negotiators probably did not know that the portage trail to bypass the falls of the Pigeon circled a few miles to the south. The treaty put the Grand Portage post on American soil!

Fearing American taxes, the North West Company decided to move the post north of the border. The Indians had long known of another route inland from Lake Superior to Rainy Lake via the Kaministikwia River. This was a more difficult route, and the voyageurs insisted on bonus pay, but it was usable.

In 1803, at great cost, the North West Company abandoned their Grand Portage stockade and moved north to build a new, bigger post, called Fort William, near the site of modern-day Thunder Bay, Ontario.

Not long after, friction between Britain and the U.S. erupted again in the War of 1812. This painting depicts the part in that war played by the North West Company schooner *Recovery.* It was an undramatic role, but one I find fascinating just the same.

When war broke out, American ships on the Great Lakes wasted no time hunting down ships used by the British fur traders. They captured the North West schooner *Mink*, sank the *Nancy*, and caused the scuttling of the *Perseverance* by her captain, Robert McCargo.

Fleeing American forces, Captain McCargo escaped to Fort William in a canoe. There, he made plans to keep their last ship, the *Recovery*, from American hands. He sailed the *Recovery* to Isle Royale and anchored her out of sight, at the end of a long bay now called McCargo Cove.

He took down her masts and covered the ship with brush and small trees to disguise her from marauding American ships. That winter she was left to freeze in, and the ship remained undetected for the duration of the war, which ended December, 1814.

Before the end of hostilities, the British Navy regained control of the upper Great Lakes. This was done by overpowering the crews of two American schooners that were lying in wait for the North West Company fur brigades on their way down from Fort William.

After the war, the *Recovery* was put into service again and resumed her duties, shuttling supplies between the Sault and Fort William.

I've spent a lot of time at McCargo Cove, trying to imagine the Recovery's peaceful existence for a few years with no companionship but the sound of trees cracking in the winter cold or the lonesome call of the raven. After awhile, would she have preferred the action of battle to her long and lonely confinement?

RECOVERY
H. SIVERTSON
©1989

H. SIVERTSON
©1990

Fishing Station on Isle Royale

After the North West Company moved north to establish Fort William, another rival, the American Fur Company, with a post located at today's Duluth, Minnesota, tried to expand north to Grand Portage in the 1820s... with little success. The Ojibway hunters of Grand Portage stayed loyal to the North West traders.

To diversify, Ramsey Crooks, owner of the American Fur Company, established the first commercial fishing stations on Lake Superior. By the 1830s, the company had fishing operations at Grand Marais and Grand Portage on the North Shore, on nearby Isle Royale, and on the South Shore at Montreal River, L'Anse, and La Pointe in the Apostle Islands.

In 1835, the American Fur Company built the 78-foot schooner *John Jacob Astor* to supply their fur-trade posts and fishing stations. The schooners *William Brewster* and *Siskawit*, and sloop *Madeline*, were soon added to the company fleet.

Lake trout, whitefish, and siscowets (also spelled siskiwit or siskawit) were found in large numbers around Isle Royale. The fur company built a series of fishing stations on the island—at Grace Harbor, Duncan Bay, Belle Island, Merritt Island, and Rock Harbor. The painting shows company headquarters on the island at Checker Point in Siskiwit Bay.

The fish were caught by Indian and *métis* fishermen, salted down in barrels, and collected from the outlying stations by the *Siskawit* and *Madeline*, to be shuttled to Rock Harbor or Checker Point. There, the barrels were picked up for delivery across the lake to La Pointe by the *Brewster* or the *Astor*.

Gabriel Franchère, an American Fur Company official, and others left brief descriptions of the Checker Point station as a collection of buildings set in a five-acre clearing, including one house of stone and four or five of logs. The structures included a residence for the head clerk, Charles Chaboillez, a house for the rest of the men, a cooper's shop, and various storehouses for supplies, salt, and fish barrels, empty and full.

Besides Chaboillez the clerk, the Checker Point station employed two coopers and seven Indian and *métis* voyageurs as fishermen. Some farm animals and gardens were kept for subsistence.

I've tried to reconstruct the scene from the limited information available. The sloop *Madeline* is loading fish barrels gathered from other island stations onto the *William Brewster* for shipment to La Pointe or the Sault. The longboat of the *Brewster* is pulled up on the shore next to the flat-bottomed skiffs used for fishing.

The group of gentlemen might include such characters of the fur trade as Gabriel Franchère of Fort Astoria fame or clerk Chaboillez. Captain John Wood of the *Brewster* and Captain Angus of the *Madeline* are undoubtedly the other gentlemen.

The venture was unsuccessful. The company sent large quantities of fish to market, but prices were poor. The economic panic of 1837-1841 eventually put an end to the American Fur Company's fishery at Isle Royale.

Mail From Nipigon

The North West Company eventually built trading posts as far west as the Pacific and north to the watersheds of the Arctic. Over one hundred such posts were established along the continent's northern waterways. Stationed at isolated sites many miles apart, the wintering managers were always starved for any news whatsoever.

Once a year, the Grand Portage rendezvous was a rare chance to exchange information in person. What furs were commanding the highest prices in Europe? Were Indian trappers taking their pelts to a rival company's post? What barter goods or prices would encourage the Indians to bring in more furs? What tricks were competition posts employing?

After the Grand Portage rendezvous dispersed each year, mail delivery between posts was a challenge. In the summer, voyageur messengers in express canoes used the familiar routes to rush news from one post to the next.

In the winter, the voyageur mailmen employed a method of transportation borrowed, like the canoe, from the Indian cultures. Dog teams were harnessed to pull sleds or *carioles*, a type of toboggan with raised sides.

Delivering mail via the "Winter Express" was not a simple undertaking. Written messages were relayed from post to post, weather permitting, from Montreal to Fort Chipewyan on Lake Athabaska, or beyond. A letter to a distant post might be delivered one year—and not answered until the next.

Experienced voyageurs who knew the routes well were selected as winter mailmen. Their decorated toboggans and dog teams reflected their colorful personalities. A speeding *cariole* pulled by dogs with jingling harness bells and bright pompons added a touch of cheer to a harsh winter landscape.

The voyageurs took great pride in their dog teams' endurance, speed, and flashy appearance. The voyageurs were known for flamboyant boasting, and their skill with a dog team was as good a topic for exaggeration as prowess with a paddle and canoe. Hair-raising escapes from thin ice and hungry wolves matched up well in a voyageur's repertoire with tales of superhuman paddling feats or running dangerous rapids.

Carrying the winter mail, a mailman faced hazards of extreme cold, blizzards, and, if he ventured out on Lake Superior, shifting ice packs. The voyageurs knew the traditional waterways best. After freeze-up in February, following Lake Superior's shoreline out on the frozen ice may have been the fastest route, if not always the safest.

A route from the Nipigon post—from the Lake Nipigon area just north of Lake Superior—to Grand Portage or Fort William may have meandered from woods to lakeshore, winding through chains of islands and crossing the ice of large inlets.

The sound of approaching harness bells must have raised the spirits of the isolated inhabitants of any fur-trade post immensely. I am sure the voyageurs and *bourgeois* gave the half-frozen mailman a warm welcome. News and parcels from across North America and possibly even from Europe made the infrequent mail-day a time for celebration.

The painting shows a voyageur driving his *cariole* across Pigeon Bay on his way to Grand Portage.

H. SIVERTSON
©1989

H. SIVERTSON
©1987

Trading en Dérouine

In the early 1800s, competition for northern furs intensified between Hudson's Bay Company, the North West Company, and a short-lived but intense rival, the XY Company.

In prime hunting territories, rival companies built posts close to each other and kept close watch on competitors' prices and tactics. The traders offered credit in advance, stocked more goods, and lowered prices. At the same time, furs in each region were getting harder to come by as animal populations were decimated by increased hunting.

Instead of waiting for the Indians to decide which post to bring their furs to, companies often sent their traders *en dérouine*. This phrase meant traveling to the Indian camps to collect furs before rivals got their hands on the precious pelts. With canoes or sledges of barter goods, traders bargained for buffalo meat and skins of beaver, lynx, wolf, and other animals.

The Indian hunters knew this competition gave them great advantages. However, the Indian families were never as eager to accumulate material goods as the traders would have wished. The traders had to adapt to the Indian ways of hunting, traveling, and trading.

From *Five Fur Traders of the Northwest*, some excerpts from the 1800-1801 diary of Archibald N. McLeod, manager of Fort Alexandria, west of Lake Winnipeg, give a hint of the winter life of voyageurs at a North West Company post.

[Dec. 21] ...the woods are cover'd with rhime [hoarfrost].... I sent Collin & Seven men off *en Derouine* to where the Vent du Nord [an Indian] came from, with [goods] for 60 skins.... [Dec. 23] ...cloudy, & the trees & everything so covered with Rhyme, that all nature seems powdered.... [Dec. 25] Being Christmass I gave the men a dram.... [Dec. 30] Collin came back [with] 19 wolves & 14 Beavers, 7 Catts, & 5 foxes, 39 bladders Grease, & a little... Meat.

[Jan. 1, 1801] Still Colder.... I gave all the people in the Fort a dram... they danced & sang all day & night, but had no quarrels.... [Jan. 4] A very fine mild day I sent off... Cadotte & Vallé to bring back the winter Express [mail].... La Voye & La Freniere went off to Hunt the Buffaloe.... [Jan. 13] ...an Indian who came here in the evening (Shagotimoh) tells us [a group of Indians camped five days march from Fort Alexandria] have got no skins, the Fort des Prairies people having lately been there en Derouine.... [Jan. 18] I am *bothered (plagued)* with a parcel of invalides... Boiselle, La Comble, Chauvin, & now Plante is unwell.... [Jan. 19] La Frenier is looking for wood to make sledges & snow shoes.... [Jan. 22] Cadieu is getting himself *tatooed* by La Frenier, as has already Boiselle.

[Feb. 1] ...Ettienne Ducharm came... to inform me there are six tents of Crees where they are [with] many Sledges load of provisions & a good many skins.... [March 3] ...Blows prodigiously, Some of the men at work... melting or Boiling back (Buffaloe) fat to put in the Pimican, all the women at work sewing Bags to put the Pimican into.... [March 18] I sent Old Parrant to make sugar at Swan River.... [April 6] Cold & blowing hard, the people are some cutting fire wood others hauling.... One of the [visiting] Shell river men having brought his Violin with him the people danced all night.

[And with the coming of spring: May 18] ...it is really incredible the quantity of water in every brook.... [May 21] ...I got the people to work at the Canoes.... [May 25] A very fine day, I made up the furs into Packs.... [May 26] Worked at the Canoes.... [May 30] ...rain very heavyly from noon untill midnight without intermission.... [May 31] Cleared up... & I sent off the Canoes [towards Grand Portage]....

With the spring brigades launched, the annual cycle of the voyageur had begun anew.

Epilogue: The End of an Era

In 1821, after years of competition, the North West Company merged with the Hudson's Bay Company. After that, the voyageur route through the Great Lakes and Border Lakes began to decline. Most of the furs were transported over shorter routes leading to Hudson Bay, which had direct access to the sea.

From 1821 until 1882, however, Hudson's Bay Company managers, survey parties, and government officials still used the voyageur canoes on occasional trips across Lake Superior to Fort William, now a Hudson's Bay post, and on to Fort Garry near Lake Winnipeg.

Artist Frances Anne Hopkins accompanied her husband, a Hudson's Bay Company official, on several long trips in voyageur canoes across portions of this route in 1864 and 1869. Her wonderfully-detailed paintings of the voyageurs, near the end of an era, give us a fascinating glimpse of these men and their canoes.

With the opening of a shipping canal at the Sault in 1855, schooners and steamships grew in number on Lake Superior. The steamer *Collingwood* was probably the first Canadian ship to pass through the locks, bound for Fort William in 1857 with a government expedition headed inland to Fort Garry.

The steamer *Rescue* began regular service along the Canadian shore, carrying mail, freight, and passengers to Fort William. The *Chicora* and *Algoma* (the first) carried voyageurs, troops, and supplies from Collingwood to Fort William for Colonel G.J. Wolseley's Red River Expedition in 1870, a punitive mission to settle a *métis* dispute over a growing pioneer settlement around Fort Garry. Wolseley traveled inland in bark canoes manned by the last of the voyageurs.

In 1882, the Canadian Pacific Railroad construction passed through Fort Garry (Winnipeg). This put an end to the need for canoe transportation inland from western Lake Superior, and Fort William closed that same year. With the closing of this post in 1882, the voyageur era of the western Great Lakes region came to an end.

Some ex-voyageurs continued to fish commercially at the abandoned American Fur Company stations around the lake and Isle Royale. Diaries of the early miners on Isle Royale in the mid-1800s mention voyageurs working as fishermen and as boat handlers serving the mining companies.

The Hudson's Bay Company remains, after over three hundred years of existence, as the oldest chartered trading company in the world. Those who claim the initials H.B.C. stand for "here before Christ" exaggerate the length of the company's empire in Canada only a little.

The colorful voyageurs in their bark canoes disappeared from the western Great Lakes without fanfare. For over 200 years, from the early 1600s to the mid-1800s, these hardworking men were the working-class backbone of one of the longest-running industries in North America. And like many other common folk, when they were no longer needed the voyageurs quickly faded from the scene, leaving few records of their lives and ways.

Except for a few diaries and far fewer pictures recording their presence, the voyageurs remain an intriguing mystery. Much of their true identity will always be left to our imagination.

Afterword

In my quest for research materials upon which to base my paintings, I was amazed and disappointed in how little visual documentation was available on the subject. One remarkable exception is a series of beautiful and descriptive voyageur paintings by Frances Anne Hopkins (1838-1919), a Victorian-era artist born in England, living in Canada in the 1860s. Married to a district manager of the Hudson's Bay Company, Hopkins made several long journeys by canoe with her husband and his voyageur employees. Captivated by the subject matter, Hopkins made a number of paintings faithfully documenting the scenes she witnessed.

Otherwise, we have few reliable images of the voyageur. Before the development of photography in the mid-1800s, galleries and publishers relied on artists to illustrate cultural and natural history. The accuracy of renderings depended on the artist's skill and knowledge of the subject. Many engravings by 18th-century artists depicting fur-trade subjects in the New World reflect a gross lack of first-hand knowledge—and rather fanciful imaginations.

Some artists of the time were specially commissioned to record historical events. They executed paintings with elegance, but with a lack of convincing detail due to their unfamiliarity with the subject. Even at the end of the voyageur era, photographers seem not to have made much of an effort to record the diminishing fur-trade culture of the western regions.

Of greater value to the researcher, a few talented employees within the fur trade made simple, yet knowledgeable sketches of their experiences. Young Peter Rindlisbacher (1806-1834) was one who produced wonderful watercolors of fur-trade activities in the Red River colony where he grew up in the early 1800s.

Adventurer and artist Paul Kane (1810-1871) traveled through the Great Lakes and western fur-trade regions in the 1840s and 1850s to document on canvas, in the manner of George Catlin, the vanishing Indian cultures of the area. From his long forays into the field, Kane's excellent portraits of Indians and their activities, painted on location, are very valuable documents. On the other hand, scenes he produced later in his studio seem more romantic and fanciful, leaving me with some reservations about their veracity.

The graceful paintings of Frances Anne Hopkins, combining her expertise as an artist with personal experiences on long canoe trips following the traditional routes, remain what I consider to be the most reliable visual record of the voyageurs, at least as they looked in the 1860s.

Luckily, the background scenery is still quite similar today. The specific points and places, the rivers and lakes, the storms and fogs are part of my own experiences growing up on Isle Royale, Lake Superior, and the North Shore. My familiarity with the local environment helped me, I hope, present the natural backdrop to the historic travels depicted here.

For further details on the activities depicted, I have combed through historical writings by such scholars as Grace Lee Nute, Harold Innis, Carolyn Gilman, Edwin Adney and Howard Chapelle, and others. I hope my work reflects well on their research and writings. Their studies have helped me in countless ways specific and general.

Certainly each historian who has not personally experienced an event is forced to borrow from the accounts and interpretations of others. Sometimes this has meant repeating an original error. The North West Company's ship, the *Otter*, is a case in point. An expert in Great Lakes maritime history identified the *Otter* as a sloop. That information was subsequently borrowed by other historians who accepted it as fact. From my research in the libraries of Old Fort William and the Grand Portage National Monument, I believe the *Otter* seen at Grand Portage in 1793 was a schooner, and I painted her that way. The arguments to support my decision are too lengthy to pursue here. I mention it only to point out that inaccurate reporting can create simple errors which are repeated until accepted as fact.

Probably the most reliable material comes from eye-witness accounts such as the diaries of participants in the actual event described. Fur traders like John Macdonell, Archibald McLeod, and others left journals outlining their everyday lives, with some description of the activities of their voyageur employees. Historians acknowledge, however, that even first-hand accounts can differ remarkably from one participant to the next.

A particularly fascinating account is John Tanner's published narrative about thirty years spent living with the Indians. As a child, Tanner was captured and traded to an Indian family which lived in the region around Grand Portage during the late 1700s. Such accounts, however, narrated to a third-party author, were sometimes sensationalized, although they clearly contain a wealth of detailed information about daily life and activities.

As an artist/historian, I tried to assemble as much information as was available from written and visual documentation. Then I went in search of the actual place involved. The following paintings are the result of many years seeking out, photographing, and sketching the natural settings that served as background for the event depicted.

Then, combining the research with my imagination and artistic tools, I sat down to build the scene on canvas or paper. By taking the canoe described by Adney and Chapelle; adding the people portrayed by the writings of Nute and the paintings of Hopkins; then setting the action in the wilderness that still exists, I tried to recreate how it may have looked.

As it slowly emerged, I too got to see at least a version of the scene for the first time. We will never know how close my interpretation is to the actual fact, but it is the best I could do with the documentation available to me. Unless proven wrong, I am willing to offer it as, perhaps, "the way it may have been."

The purpose of interpretation is not solely to present facts but to help us see, imagine, and try to understand. I hope my paintings will let you experience a hint of the life of the voyageur canoemen.

In a similar vein, I highly recommend a visit to today's reconstructed fur-trade posts. Colorful re-enactments of voyageur's rendezvous and the daily life of a fur-trade post take place at historical sites at Grand Portage in northern Minnesota, Old Fort William in Thunder Bay, Ontario, and Fort Michilimackinac on the northern tip of Michigan. These sites and their visitor programs are carefully developed from archeological, written, and visual records.

I enjoy telling stories with my art, and am presently working on a third volume to fill in some of the gap between the era of *The Illustrated Voyageur* and the more recent period depicted in *Once Upon An Isle.*

The original paintings reproduced in *The Illustrated Voyageur* were done either in watercolor or in oil. Most of the early paintings are watercolors, while the later ones are done in oils.

For those interested, my current paintings can be found at the Sivertson Gallery in Grand Marais, Minnesota. Some of the scenes are also available as limited or open-edition prints.

Further Resources

Selected Museums

Grand Portage National Monument
P.O. Box 666
Grand Marais, Minnesota 55604
(tel. 218-387-2788)
Stockade open daily mid-May to mid-October. The historic site of the Grand Portage post, with reconstructed stockade and Great Hall, exhibits, demonstrations, video program.

Old Fort William
Vickers Heights PO
Thunder Bay, Ontario P0T 2Z0, Canada
(tel. 807-577-8461)
Open daily year-round; expanded activities mid-June to mid-August. With dozens of costumed interpreters in summer season recreating the life of a fur-trade post during rendezvous. Guided tours, canoe activities, dramatic re-enactments, craft and trade demonstrations.

Colonial Michilimackinac
Mackinac State Historical Parks
P.O. Box 370
Mackinac Island, MI 49757
(tel. 906-847-3328)
Open daily mid-May to mid-October. This state park at the northern tip of lower Michigan recreates the historic Great Lakes fur-trade post of the 1770s. Guided tours, military and craft demonstrations.

Lower Fort Garry
Box 37, Group 343, RR3
Selkirk, Manitoba R1A 2A8, Canada
(tel. 204-785-6050)
Open daily mid-May to Labor Day. Near Winnipeg, this historic Hudson's Bay Company site portrays a fur-trade post of the 1850s.

Books on Voyageur History

Edwin T. Adney and Howard I. Chapelle. *The Bark Canoes and Skin Boats of North America.* Washington, DC: Smithsonian Institution, 1964. An in-depth study of these historic watercraft, with numerous illustrations.

John J. Bigsby. *The Shoe and Canoe*; or, *Pictures of Travel in the Canadas.* 2 volumes. London: Chapman & Hall, 1850. An interesting collection of notes and sketches of life and travel in Canada in the mid-1800s.

Janet E. Clark and Robert Stacey. *Francis Anne Hopkins 1838-1919: Canadian Scenery.* Thunder Bay: Thunder Bay Art Gallery, 1990. An important catalog of the paintings of Hopkins depicting voyageur travels and landscapes.

Charles M. Gates, ed. *Five Fur Traders of the Northwest.* St. Paul: Minnesota Historical Society, 1965. Fascinating first-hand diaries by traders John Macdonell, Archibald N. McLeod, and others.

Carolyn Gilman. *The Grand Portage Story.* St. Paul: Minnesota Historical Society Press, 1992. An insightful history of 300 years of trade and tradition involving the Grand Portage post. Highly recommended.

Carolyn Gilman. *Where Two Worlds Meet: The Great Lakes Fur Trade.* St. Paul: Minnesota Historical Society, 1982. An exhibition catalog, with guest essays, showing the interaction of Indian and European cultures.

Harold A. Innis. *The Fur Trade in Canada: An Introduction to Canadian Economic History.* Revised edition. Toronto: University of Toronto Press, 1973. A key study of the economic history of the fur trade.

Grace Lee Nute. *The Voyageur.* St. Paul: Minnesota Historical Society, 1931. An engaging portrait of the French-Canadian canoemen and their songs and customs.

Grace Lee Nute. *The Voyageur's Highway: Minnesota's Border Lake Land.* St Paul: Minnesota Historical Society, 1951. A historical guide to the Minnesota-Ontario canoe country, from Lake Superior to Rainy Lake.

Eric W. Morse. *Fur Trade Canoe Routes of Canada: Then and Now.* Minocqua, WI: NorthWord Press, 1984. First published in 1969, this book retraces key routes for modern-day canoeists, with a good overview of fur-trade history and cultural geography.

John Tanner. *A Narrative of the Captivity and Adventures of John Tanner.* Reprint of 1830 original. New York and London: Garland Publishing, 1975. A fascinating account of growing up in an Indian family circa 1790-1820.

Periodicals

The Beaver: Exploring Canada's History. Published bi-monthly by the Hudson's Bay Company. 450 Portage Avenue, Winnipeg, Manitoba R3C 0E7, Canada. (tel. 204-786-7048)

For Younger Readers

Ellen Green. "Fur Trade" (*Roots Magazine*, Vol. 10, No. 1 Fall). St. Paul: Minnesota Historical Society, 1981. 31-page booklet.

Traditional Music

12 Voyageur Songs. Audio cassette, with 25-page companion booklet by Theodore C. Blegen. St. Paul: Minnesota Historical Society, 1966. Traditional songs in French by a choir from New Brunswick, Canada.